FORTNITE BATTLE ROYALE HACKS

ADVANCED STRATEGIES

D0727225

FORTNITE BATTLE ROYALE HACKS

ADVANCED STRATEGIES

THE UNOFFICAL GUIDE TO TIPS AND TRICKS THAT OTHER GUIDES WON'T TEACH YOU

JASON R. RICH

STUDIO PRESS

STUDIO PRESS BOOKS

First published in the UK in 2018 by Studio Press Books,
an imprint of Kings Road Publishing,
part of Bonnier Books UK,
The Plaza, 535 King's Road, London, SW10 0SZ
www.studiopressbooks.co.uk
www.bonnierbooks.co.uk

Copyright © 2018 by Sky Pony Press

10 9 8 7 6 5 4 3

Fortnite® is a registered trademark of Epic Games, Inc.

The Fortnite game is copyright © Epic Games, Inc.

*Screenshots from Fortnite Battle Royale © Epic Games, Inc. All rights reserved.

This book is not official; it is not authorized, endorsed or sponsored by Epic Games, Inc. or any other person
or entity owning or controlling rights in the Fortnite Battle Royale names, trademarks, or copyright.
Portions of the materials used are trademarks and/or copyrighted works of Epic Games, Inc.
All rights reserved by Epic

All rights reserved. No part of this book may be reproduced in any manner without the express written
consent of the publisher, except in the case of brief excerpts in critical reviews or articles. All inquiries
should be addressed to Sky Pony Press, 307 West 36th Street, 11th Floor, New York, NY 10018.

A CIP catalogue record for this book is available from the British Library.

Paperback ISBN: 978-1-78741-451-8
Ebook ISBN: 978-1-78741-475-4

Written by Jason R. Rich
Cover designed by Brian Peterson

Printed in the United Kingdom

TABLE OF CONTENTS

SECTION 1

WELCOME TO THE ISLAND: DISCOVER WHAT'S NEW

Ask any gamer what the most popular game in the world is right now, and chances are, they'll tell you it's **Fortnite: Battle Royale!**

© Epic Games, Inc.

In addition to offering exciting and challenging gameplay, this game allows players to compete in real-time against up to 99 others during each exciting and action-packed match.

Game publisher Epic Games has done an amazing job keeping players interested in Fortnite: Battle Royale by continuously introducing new features, gameplay elements, and content. This continuous game evolution makes it even more interesting, fun to play, and increasingly challenging to master.

What You Need to Get Started Playing

Fortnite: Battle Royale is a massively multiplayer online game that's available for Windows PC, Mac, PlayStation 4, Xbox One, iPhone, iPad, and Android-based mobile device. A Nintendo Switch version is rumored to be in development for release in late 2018.

To download the game if you're a PC or Mac computer user, visit www.Fortnite.com (shown above) and click on the yellow Get Fortnite button (found near the bottom-center of the screen). PlayStation 4 users should visit the PlayStation Store, while Xbox One users should visit the Xbox Marketplace.

The iOS mobile device version of the game (shown on the previous page on an iPad Pro) is available from the Apple App Store, while the Android-based version of the game (when it becomes available) can be acquired from the Google Play Store.

A continuous Internet connection is required. If you're playing on a PC or Mac, or any mobile device, you'll also need a free Epic Games account. PlayStation 4 gamers require a PlayStation Network account, while a paid membership to Xbox Gold is required for Xbox One users.

Sound Plays an Integral Part in the Game

The sounds you hear within the game can help you achieve success, so always listen carefully. For example, when an adversary is nearby, you'll hear their footsteps, especially when you're both inside a building. Plus, based on the sound of weapon fire, it's often possible to determine how far away you are from an enemy, and from which direction they're attacking.

If someone is collecting resources using their pickaxe, this, too, makes noise, especially if they're collecting metal by smashing cars or trucks. When you're the one collecting resources, make sure you're alone in the area. However, if you hear the sound of someone else collecting resources, this means they don't have a weapon in hand, so consider launching a sneak attack or using a projectile weapon, such as agrenade, to defeat them.

The Cost for Playing Fortnite: Battle Royale

The core Fortnite: Battle Royale game is totally free! For some gaming platforms, however, you can purchase the complete Battle Royale game, which includes story-based "Save the World" missions, but these offer a totally separate gameplay experience from Fortnite: Battle Royale.

As a Fortnite: Battle Royale player using any gaming platform, you're given the option to purchase V-Bucks (using real money), which can be exchanged for Battle Passes, as well as items from the Item Shop that allow you to customize your character's appearance in the game.

Character customizations have zero impact on a character's fighting ability, speed, strength, aim, or agility within the game. The customizations you make to your character are for appearance purposes only. Many gamers, however, take great pride in creating a fun and unique look for their soldiers.

By completing daily or weekly challenges, completing objectives in Battle Passes, or by redeeming offers from Epic Games's promotional partners, it's possible to acquire customization items for your soldier, and unlock other loot.

If you're an Amazon Prime member and have a Twitch.tv account, periodically free game items are made available for download. These are called Twitch Prime Packs. To learn more, visit www.twitch.tv/prime/fortnite.

Overview of the Game

Almost all of the action in Fortnite: Battle Royale takes place on a mysterious island. The island itself is divided into more than 20 unique points of interest. At the start of each match, you find yourself in the pre-deployment area with many other soldiers. This is where you wait for other players to join the match before it begins.

You and 99 other soldiers are then forced to climb aboard a Battle Bus (a blue bus that flies) to be transported to the island.

Once the bus begins to fly over the island (shown on the previous page), jump out at any time to free fall toward land. You choose when to leap off the bus and where your landing spot will be. As you're in free fall, control the direction your soldier travels. This allows you to traverse more than half the island, if necessary, while in midair.

© Epic Games, Inc.

Each soldier who leaps off the Battle Bus is equipped with a Glider. Once activated, the glider slows your rate of descent and gives you additional navigational control, so you can choose a precise landing spot on the island. During free fall, activate the Glider at any time. However, if you wait too long, the glider activates itself as you get close to land.

© Epic Games, Inc.

Once you set foot on the island, you'll quickly discover that you're stranded there with up to 99 enemy soldiers. You're armed only with a pickaxe (shown on the previous page). Your first two objectives are to find and grab at least one weapon, and to choose a strategy for survival.

The ultimate goal in Fortnite: Battle Royale is survival! Out of the up to 100 soldiers that land on the island during a match, you need to survive and become the last person alive. Sound simple? Well, it's not! Up to 99 other soldiers want to defeat you, and there's a deadly storm to contend with.

© Epic Games, Inc.

Except for the other soldiers on the island, you'll quickly discover that the island is deserted. The buildings (Tilted Towers is shown here), homes, stores, barns, mines, mansions, factories, bases, cars, trucks, towers, and other structures are all empty. What you will find within each point of interest are a selection of weapons, ammo, and loot to collect and use to help your survival efforts. Of course, you'll also likely encounter enemy soldiers who want to end you.

© Epic Games, Inc.

There's also an abundance of resources (wood, stone, and metal) to find and collect. These resources are used to build custom walls, structures, ramps, stairs, and fortresses. Use your pickaxe to gather resources or keep an eye out for bundles of resources on the ground.

© Epic Games, Inc.

Resources can also be used at Vending Machines that are scattered throughout the island to purchase rare and powerful weapons or loot.

The Pros and Cons of Fighting

From the moment you land on the island, you could quickly find shelter; try to avoid all enemy soldiers; collect weapons, ammo, and loot; and spend your time exploring the island. However, as a match progresses, if you manage to stay alive, eventually you'll be forced to fight.

Yet another option is to immediately go on the offensive. As soon as you land, grab some weapons, ammo, and loot, and then engage in battle with as many enemy soldiers as you can find. Your experience level in the game will increase with each victory. However, your ultimate goal is to be the last person standing. Even if you're the second-to-last person who remains alive during a match, once you're defeated, it's still game over for you.

Each time you engage in battle with any enemy soldier, there are serious risks. For example, he or she could be more experienced, or be armed with a more diverse and powerful arsenal of weapons. Their HP and Shield meters could be maxed out (meaning they can withstand more damage), or they could be better at quickly building protective walls or fortresses. In addition, every gamer improves their fighting and survival abilities with practice, so your adversary might have faster reflexes, skill, and better aim (when shooting a weapon) than you.

There's Also a Deadly Storm to Contend With

At the same moment you land on the island, a deadly storm begins to form. Don't get caught in the storm for too long, or you'll perish! If you need to escape quickly, and you need to cover a lot of territory in order to reach a safe area of the island, consider using a Launch Pad, if you have one available.

© Epic Games, Inc.

Initially, the entire island is safe and inhabitable. This is what the island map looks like just after you land on the island. However, after a short time, the deadly storm will materialize.

© Epic Games, Inc.

Slowly at first, the deadly storm makes portions of the island uninhabitable. The storm continues to move and expand, until only a small circular area remains safe. If you survive this long, it's within this small circular area where the final battles (known as the End Game) will take place—leaving only one solider alive.

© Epic Games, Inc.

The on-screen timer will inform you about when the next storm will once again expand and move. When it's about to expand, you'll hear the sound of a timer ticking, hear and see the storm approaching, and see a warning message appear near the center of the screen.

On the island map, the area of the island that the storm has taken over is displayed in pink. The clear area inside the white circle is the inhabitable (safe) area.

Each match lasts approximately 15 minutes. During this time, the storm will move and expand several times. It's important that you pay careful attention to the storm's progression. Stay in the inhabitable areas of the island (within the circle), as much as possible.

© Epic Games, Inc.

While you can enter the storm for a short time, your HP (Health Points) and Shields will get depleted, slowly at first, but at a faster pace the longer you stay in the storm. You'll also receive more damage when you go inside the storm later in matches. Walking or even running while stuck inside the storm is a slow process. If you wind up in a part of the island that's very far from the safe area, you might not be able to escape before your HP and Shields are fully depleted. Your position on the map is displayed as a white triangle icon. If you do get stuck in the storm, follow the white line on the map to safety. It's displayed on the map in the upper-right corner of the screen.

© Epic Games, Inc.

Should you find yourself stuck in a storm and you have a Launch Pad in your backpack, build a platform on the ground, place the Launch Pad on top of it, activate it, and then step on it. You'll be catapulted into the air. Your glider will activate, and you'll be able to sail a good distance, hopefully directly toward a safe area. If a Jetpack is available, use it to help you escape the storm quickly.

Fortnite: Battle Royale's GamePlay Modes

In Fortnite: Battle Royale, there are several main gameplay modes. Periodically, additional gameplay modes become available, some for just a limited time. When this happens, a message about it appears in the Lobby prior to a match.

© Epic Games, Inc.

From the Lobby, choose which gameplay mode to experience. Options include: **Solo** (it's you against up to 99 other players), **Duos** (pair up with a friend and defeat up to 98 other soldiers), or **Squads** (invite up to three friends to team up with you, and fight against up to 96 enemy soldiers).

Once you choose Duos or Squads, invite friends to join you from the Lobby. All versions of Fortnite: Battle Royale are cross-platform compatible, so while you may be playing on a Windows PC, for example, you can team up with players using a PS4, an Xbox One, a Mac, or a mobile device.

Experience Seasons in Fortnite

Every two weeks or so, Epic Games releases a game update. This might include new weapons, loot, or challenges. To learn about the latest updates, visit www.epicgames.com/fortnite/en-UK/news.

Every few months, however, a new Season of gameplay kicks off. This involves a major game update, which typically includes alternate versions of the island, with the introduction of new points of interest and drastic changes to established points of interest. New weapons and loot items are also introduced, along with a selection of themed soldier outfits and accessories. A new Battle Pass also becomes available.

What You Should Know About Battle Passes

At the start of each Season, a new Battle Pass becomes available. For a fee, gamers can purchase an optional Battle Pass, which includes a series of daily and weekly challenges.

In addition to completing daily and weekly challenges, as well as tiers in the current Battle Pass, you will earn Experience Points (XP) by winning battles and accomplishing other achievements during each match.

Current challenges are displayed on the game's Lobby screen. Here, they're displayed on the left side of the screen, below the character's Level information.

Once you pay for a Battle Pass, from the Lobby, access the Battle Pass screen to discover each tier of challenges that await, and discover what prizes will be unlocked. You can also purchase a Battle Pass from here.

Each time you accomplish one or more of these challenges, new and exclusive loot, character outfits, character accessories, emotes, Experience Point (XP) boosts, unique skydiving trails, spray paint icons, new banner designs, up to 100 V-bucks (which can be used for new loot purchases), or other cosmetic items are unlocked.

Without paying for a Battle Pass, gamers can experience free challenges, but the loot you'll unlock and earn when you complete them is nowhere near as awesome or exclusive. Nothing you unlock by completing challenges offered by a Battle Pass, however, actually improves your soldier's strength, agility, speed, aim, or fighting ability.

© Epic Games, Inc.

If you want to unlock prizes without actually completing the challenges, purchase (using V-Bucks, which cost real money) the ability to unlock Battle Pass Tiers and collect the loot automatically.

What's New in Fortnite

Since Fortnite: Battle Royale is continuously evolving thanks to game updates from Epic Games, you can expect to see new points of interest on the map, new character outfits, new weapons, as well as new types of loot available to you, beyond what you'll read about in this unofficial strategy guide which was written during Season 4.

© Epic Games, Inc.

During Season 4 (which kicked off in May 2018), the island was pummeled by comets from outer space. Craters began appearing throughout the island. The largest comet destroyed the area formally known as **Dusty Dunes**, and in its place, **Dusty Divot** was build. (As seen on the previous page.

In addition, new points of interest, including Risky Reels (a drive-in movie theater), were added to the island, along with some awesome new weapons and loot items.

This unofficial strategy guide is chock-full of tips for avoiding the storm, exploring the island, surviving battles against enemy soldiers, and ultimately, winning matches. While knowing these strategies will help you immensely, nothing replaces the need to practice.

The more time you spend actually playing Fortnite: Battle Royale, the easier it will be to work with the various weapons, maneuver your soldier, and utilize the various tools (loot) available to you. Plus, you'll speed up your ability to quickly build walls, ramps, stairs, and fortresses, that'll help keep you alive.

© Epic Games, Inc.

Each Season introduces new mysteries and storylines that don't always get resolved right away. For example, during Season 4, this mysterious hatch in the ground appeared within Wailing Woods. The hatch could not be opened, smashed, or altered in any way. Its purpose will likely be revealed during Season 5 or beyond.

SECTION 2
CUSTOMIZING YOUR CONTROLLER SETTINGS & CHARACTER

Starting from the Lobby screen before each match, Fortnite: Battle Royale allows you to customize your controller (or keyboard/ mouse) options. Whether or not you tweak these options is a matter of personal preferences. It's not a requirement. Meanwhile, from the Locker screen, you're able to customize the appearance of your solder, assuming you've unlocked or purchased outfits and related content.

Adjusting Your Wireless Controller (Keyboard/Mouse) Settings

The default controller (or keyboard/mouse) settings offered by the game work well for most players as they first start playing Fortnite: Battle Royale. However, based on personal preferences that you'll develop while playing the game, you may opt to tweak the controller settings. To do this, from the Lobby screen, access the games Options menu and the select the gear-shaped Settings menu.

Game

Matchmaking Region	◄ Asia ►	
Input		
Mouse Sensitivity	.28	
Wireless Controller Sensitivity X	5	
Wireless Controller Sensitivity Y	5	
Mouse ADS Sensitivity	1.00	
Mouse Scope Sensitivity	1.00	
Wireless Controller ADS Sensitivit	.65	
/ireless Controller Scope Sensitivit	.65	
Invert View	◄ Off ►	
Camera and Display		
Streamer Mode	◄ Off ►	

Global   Hold to chat   Reset Game To Default   Back
© Epic Games, Inc.

The main Settings menu is comprised of six sub-menus labeled Game, Brightness Calibration, Audio, Color Correction, Input (for Keyboard/Mouse controls), Wireless Controller, and Account.

In the Game menu, it's possible to adjust options like Wireless Controller or Mouse Sensitivity. By scrolling down on this menu, you can turn on/off options like Toggle Targeting, Aim Assist, Turbo Building, Auto Material Change, and Controller Auto-Run, each of which directly impacts some aspect of the control you'll have over your character during a match.

It's important to see and hear everything within the game. Based on the room lighting where you're playing and the brightness of your screen, consider manually adjusting the Brightness Calibration and sound-related options (shown on the previous page).. For example, you may opt to turn up the Sound FX Volume option but turn down the Music Volume and Voice Chat Volume, since clearly hearing sounds effects in the game, like footsteps and weapons fire, is crucial.

Based on the overall strategies and approach to the game you choose to adopt, by adjusting the Wireless Controller (or Keyboard/Mouse) options, it's possible to make the commands and functions you use the most, the easiest to access. For example, the Standard (or "Old School") wireless controller layout (shown on a PS4) focuses on the most commonly used gaming features.

The Quick Builder (shown at the bottom of the previous page on a PS4) controller layout puts more emphasis on basic building.

The Builder Pro controller layout (shown on the PS4) emphasizes controls used primarily for advanced building, while the Combat Pro layout makes fighting-related functions easiest to access.

If you watch a YouTube video or Twitch.tv live stream in which an expert Fortnite player talks about their controller (or keyboard/mouse) settings, the settings they talk about work for them personally, based on their motor skills, muscle memory, and their personal tastes they've developed while playing Fortnite: Battle Royale for countless hours.

Only adjust options that allow gameplay elements to work better for you personally, which you'll discover mainly through experimentation and experience. Don't just copy someone else's Settings adjustments, unless you have a good reason to do so.

Customize the Appearance of Your Soldier

There are several customizations you can make to the appearance of your soldier. Start by choosing his or her outfit. This is the clothing worn during a match. You're also able to select separate back bling, which determines the appearance of their backpack.

Next, choose the design of their glider (and related free-fall/Contrail animation), the appearance of their pickaxe, and what emotes (including dance moves) they can publically showcase during a match.

Remember, the customizations you make to your solider only impact how he/she looks in the game. You can spend real money to make your soldier appear truly awesome and unique, but this is optional.

Most gamers really appreciate the ability to customize the appearance of their soldiers. For example, you can select their outfits, back bling, glider design, pickaxe design, free fall trail animation, loading screen graphic, banner, emotes, and spray paint tag designs. Customizing your soldier's appearance can be done before each match. From the Lobby screen, access the Locker screen, and then choose the Outfit option (shown here). Only outfits you've unlocked, previously acquired, or purchased will be displayed.

The options available to you are what you unlock during gameplay, what you purchase from the Item Shop, and what you download (for free) from Epic Game's promotional partners. Items from the Item Shop are purchased one at a time using V-Bucks.

If you select the Glider option from the Locker screen, a selection of the Glider designs you've unlocked, purchased, or acquired are displayed. Choose one from the menu and confirm your choice.

Every day, a new selection of customizable options (including outfits, glider designers, pickaxe designs, and emotes), are available for sale from the Item Shop. Purchase one item at a time by exchanging V-Bucks. These items cost real money and are typically only available for a very limited time.

Plan on spending between £5.00 and £25.00 for a single outfit, or more if you want to add matching back bling and a pickaxe, for example. This optional Whiplash outfit, for example, costs 800 V-Bucks. Click on the Store menu option to purchase V-Bucks that you can exchange for items or Battle Passes. Purchasing 1,000 V-Bucks costs £7.99. It would be cheaper, however, to use V-Bucks you've won within the game, or to purchase 2,800 (£19.99), 7,500 (£49.99), or 13,500 (£79.99) V-Bucks at once. These figures are approximate at the time of publication.

SECTION 3
FORTNITE GEOGRAPHY: GET TO KNOW THE ISLAND

It's important that you discover how and when to access the island map, and that you learn how to identify key locations on the map. The island is composed of 20+ points of interest, including several new and popular destinations, which are not labeled on the map.

© Epic Games, Inc.

While you're in the pre-deployment area waiting to board the Battle Bus, or while the Battle Bus is in the air, access the island map. A blue line (composed of arrows) displays the random route the Battle Bus will take over the island, so you can more easily decide when to leave the bus and choose a preferred landing site.

While viewing the island map that shows the route that the Battle Bus will follow, start thinking about your desired landing location. Do you want to land in a less popular and more secluded area, so you can gather weapons and resources, or would you prefer to drop down into a popular part of the island, where you're sure to encounter enemy soldiers and be forced to fight almost immediately?

© Epic Games, Inc.

Suppose your desired landing spot is Shabby Shores (located near map coordinates A5), but when you look at the island map that shows the route the Battle Bus will take, its route takes you nowhere near this area. Now what? As with all points of interest, even if the route the Battle Bus takes does not travel directly over your desired landing location, you can move during free fall more than halfway across the entire island before your soldier's glider automatically deploys. As a result, you can almost always reach any area on the map.

© Epic Games, Inc.

At any time during a match, access the full-screen island map to figure out where you are, where you want to go, and the location of the storm. As you can see on the previous page, the portion of the island that's engulfed in the storm (and uninhabitable) is displayed in pink. The safe area is within the circle.

How to Read the Island Map

The full island map is divided into quadrants (boxes). Displayed along the top margin of the map (from left to right) are the letters "A" through "J". Along the left margin of the map, from top to bottom, are the numbers "1" through "10." Using these letters and numbers, you can easily identify any location or quadrant on the map.

For example, quadrant F2 on the map corresponds with Anarchy Acres, while coordinates H6 correspond with Retail Row. Lucky Landing can be found in quadrant G10.

© Epic Games, Inc.

When you see two circles on the map, the outer (larger) circle represents the safe area of the island right now. The inner white circle shows where the safe area will be once the storm moves and expands again.

© Epic Games, Inc.

On the main game screen during a match, a small map is always displayed. It shows your current location. If you're outside the safe area, follow the white line that's displayed on this smaller map to reach safety as quickly as possible. Run! If you have a Launch Pad or Jetpack available, use it to make your escape and cover a lot of territory fast.

Choose the Best Moment to Jump from the Battle Bus

© Epic Games, Inc.

At the start of each match, choose when to jump off the Battle Bus as it sails across the sky, directly over the island (as seen on the previous page.)

Once you leave the Battle Bus, your soldier free falls toward the island, but you can control the speed and direction they're falling. If you don't touch the controller, your soldier falls at a steady pace. Remember, the soldiers that make it safely to the ground first are at an advantage, because they can quickly grab a weapon and then start shooting unarmed adversaries as they land.

If you point your soldier downward during free fall, their falling speed increases dramatically, allowing them to reach land faster (as seen on the previous page.). If you wait too long to deploy the glider, however, it activates automatically to ensure a safe landing.

© Epic Games, Inc.

Once a glider is active, it slows a soldier's falling speed. Plus, you have more precise control over your soldier's movement during the final portion of their decent.

© Epic Games, Inc.

If you're landing in or near any point of interest (or known structure), land directly on the roof of a house, building, or structure (as seen in the previous page.) Sometimes, you'll find weapons, ammo, or loot to collect out in the open, lying on the roof. Upon landing, smash through the roof to the attic of a house, or the top floor of a building or tower. You'll often find a chest in these high-up areas, so you can quickly arm yourself before encountering enemy soldiers.

Need Directions? Check the Map

The small map that's continuously displayed on the screen and the full-size map both offer a lot of useful information when it comes to navigation and determining the safest places to go to avoid the deadly storm.

© Epic Games, Inc.

When a white line appears within the small map, this is the path to follow to avoid the moving storm. If you see a portion of the white circle displayed within this small map, this indicates that you're close to the border of uninhabitable area due to the storm. If you find yourself outside this circle once the storm moves, it's not a good situation.

© Epic Games, Inc.

Using the full-size map, figure out where you want to go next, as well as the best route to follow, based on the direction the storm is moving, and which area of the island you want to reach. Remember, the inner white circle on the map indicates where the safe area will be after the storm moves again.

© Epic Games, Inc.

If you're defeated, don't despair. Stick around for a bit and take advantage of Spectator Mode. This allows you to kick back and watch other players compete in the match you were just eliminated from.

Simply by watching other gamers explore, you'll learn a lot about various regions of the map and discover new strategies to use when engaged in fights.

Choose Your Landing Destination Like A Pro

If you watch live streams (on YouTube or Twitch.tv) of the top-ranked Fortnite players in the world, one strategy you'll often see them implement is choosing a very remote place to land once their soldier jumps from the Battle Bus. They'll further choose a landing location they know offers multiple chests that can be found and opened within moments of landing.

Anytime you choose a landing spot that's as far away as possible from the flyover route taken by the Battle Bus, and that is not near the very beginning or end of its route, you'll typically be able to land in an area that's not heavily populated with enemies. In some cases, you'll wind up alone in the area. This gives you more time to gather weapons and resources.

© Epic Games, Inc.

One ideal landing location for this strategy is between map coordinates I2.5 and J2.5 (outside of Wailing Woods) (shown in the previous page.) Land on top of this house that contains a tall wooden tower on top of it. Smash your way downward using the pickaxe.

© Epic Games, Inc.

You'll discover at least two chests here.

© Epic Games, Inc.

There are also weapons, ammo, and loot to grab directly from the ground. Be sure to explore the house itself.

Chances are, you won't be able to spend too much time in this area due to the storm, but collect what you can to establish your arsenal, plus collect nearby resources.

Instead of spending time visiting the island's various points of interest, determine where the storm is headed by looking at the map, and avoid enemy soldiers early on in the match by staying exclusively in the outskirts of those popular island locations.

© Epic Games, Inc.

Along the way, visit small structures that are outside of the points of interest to collect additional weapons, ammo, and loot.

Even if you avoid points of interest, you'll likely encounter a few enemy soldiers. You can choose to fight or avoid them. As the storm continues to expand, focus on staying within the safe circle, while building your arsenal and resource collection. Do this before the circle gets really small, and you're forced to fight the remaining enemy soldiers during the End Game.

Using this strategy helps to ensure you collect the weapons and resources you will need for the final battles in a match, plus it keeps you out of potentially dangerous and crowded points of interest on the map.

Among the other potential landing sites that allow you to pursue this strategy include a home found at map coordinates A6, or the llama-shaped wooden tower outside of Junk Junction (near map coordinates B1).

Discover the Island's Hotspots

The following is a summary of the island's important hotspots. For more information on these, as well as other important places to visit, I suggest grabbing a copy of "Fortnite Battle Royale Secrets of the Island".

ANARCHY ACRES (Map Coordinates: F3)

This is one of two farm areas on the island. It contains barns, silos, tractors, a farmhouse, and a bunch of crop fields.

DUSTY DIVOT (Map Coordinates: G5)

This is the area once known as Dusty Dunes. At the start of Season 4, it was demolished by a comet. The problem with this area is that it's centrally located on the map and very popular. As a result, you'll definitely encounter many enemy soldiers here, so be ready to fight.

FATAL FIELDS (Map Coordinates: G8.5)

As you explore this region, you'll discover that it's a second, rather large farming area. The farmhouse, silos, barn, and stable, as well as the farm's other structures, are far apart. To reach each of them, you'll need to spend time out in the open and will be vulnerable to attack. Be prepared to hide behind objects, or build walls to use as shields, in case you're attacked.

© Epic Games, Inc.

FLUSH FACTORY (Map Coordinates: D9.5)

This is an abandoned, multi-level toilet factory. Inside, explore the manufacturing area, as well as the offices and restrooms. There's plenty of useful loot to find and gather inside.

© Epic Games, Inc.

GREASY GROVE (Map Coordinates: C7)

Fast food restaurants, a few stores, and homes are what you'll encounter in this region of the island.

© Epic Games, Inc.

HAUNTED HILLS (Map Coordinates: B3)

The churches, crypts, and graveyard in this relatively small region provide an ideal setting for shootouts. There's also great scavenging to be done here for chests, weapons, ammo, loot, and stone.

© Epic Games, Inc.

JUNK JUNCTION (Map Coordinates: Between B1.5 and C1.5)
Junk cars and garbage are piled up everywhere within Junk Junction. You'll often find items to collect on top of car and garbage piles. On the ground, between the piles, is a maze-like area to explore.

© Epic Games, Inc.

LONELY LODGE (Map Coordinates: J5)
You may think of camping as a relaxing activity. However, it's anything but relaxing here in Lonely Lodge, where you'll find a lodge, a collection of cabins, parked RVs, and a tall observation tower.

© Epic Games, Inc.

LOOT LAKE (Map Coordinates: E4)

In the middle of the lake, there's an island that contains a house. Inside, you'll discover chests and other useful items to collect. Then, make your way to the rowboat in the center of the lake, as well as the buildings (located near docks) on the opposite side of the lake.

LUCKY LANDING (Map Coordinates: Between F10 and G10)

In the building that contains the giant pink tree, you might find rare and powerful weapons. Be sure to explore all of the buildings, bridges, and towers in this region.

MOISTY MIRE (Map Coordinates: I9)

This region contains lots of trees that make up a dense forest. Located near the outskirts of Moisty Mire is an abandoned prison.

PLEASANT PARK (Map Coordinates: C3)

In addition to Snobby Shores, this is an area of the island that contains a bunch of single-family homes. There's also a park and sports field here.

RETAIL ROW (Map Coordinates: H6)

This area contains a handful of shops, restaurants, a water tower and a few homes, most of which surround street parking areas. One of the unique things about this region is that chests are not always found in the same place.

RISKY REELS (Map Coordinates: H2)

This is one of the new points of interest added to the map in conjunction with Season 4. Here, you'll find a drive-in movie theater. In the parking lot are a bunch of abandoned cars and trucks.

SALTY SPRINGS (Map Coordinates: F7)

A group of single-family homes and a gas station are clustered together in this area. Be sure to search the homes, but be on the lookout for enemy soldiers who may be lurking within them.

SHIFTY SHAFTS (Map Coordinates: D7)

In addition to the buildings and structures you can see above ground, this region contains a maze-like collection of underground mining tunnels.

SNOBBY SHORES (Map Coordinates: A5)

This area contains several lovely waterfront mansions with many rooms to explore. Located near this region are two mountains. In Season 4, one mountain has a secret base hidden inside it, while the other contains a home. (This base may be removed from the game in Season 5 or later.)

© Epic Games, Inc.

TILTED TOWERS (Map Coordinates: D5.5)

Tilted Towers is one of the most popular places on the island, so you're sure to encounter many enemy soldiers here. Be prepared to fight your way through each of the buildings. Also, be ready to protect yourself when you're on the ground walking or running on the roads.

© Epic Games, Inc.

TOMATO TOWN (Map Coordinates: G4)

Aside from a pizza restaurant, taco stand, and gas station, this area contains several homes to explore. The interesting parts of this point of interest are the tunnels and bridges that lead into and out of this region.

WAILING WOODS (Map Coordinates: I3)

Here, be sure to collect plenty of wood using your pickaxe. In the center of this area is a hedge maze. Make your way through the maze to discover wooden structures that contain items worth collecting.

© Epic Games, Inc.

SECTION 4

THERE'S AN ARSENAL OF WEAPONS AVAILABLE ON THE ISLAND

At any given time, the island contains hundreds of different types of weapons to collect, store in your backpack, and then use against adversaries.

The weapon categories these firearms and explosives typically fall into include: Assault Rifles, Crossbows, Grenade Launchers, Grenades, Miniguns, Pistols, Rocket Launchers, Shotguns, SMGs (Sub Machine Guns), and Sniper Rifles.

© Epic Games, Inc.

© Epic Games, Inc.

Many Fortnite gamers agree that the most useful weapon to master is any type of shotgun. There are many types to choose from, and shotguns are more powerful than pistols. When you view the Backpack Inventory screen, details about the selected weapon/item you're holding are displayed. Here, details about the Tactical Shotgun are displayed.

Shotguns can be used in close-range or mid-range combat situations, or even at a distance. (From a distance, they're harder to aim accurately than a rifle with a scope, for example.) When using a shotgun, always try for a headshot to inflict the most damage.

Each category of weapon can be used for a different purpose. Based on the type of enemy encounter you're experiencing at any given moment, it's essential that you choose the most appropriate weapon at your disposal.

Before engaging in a firefight, consider:

- The types of weapons currently in your backpack and available to you.
- The amount of ammo you currently have for each weapon. (Be sure to pick up as much ammo as you can throughout each match.)
- The distance between you and your opponent.
- Your surroundings, and whether or not your weapon will need to destroy a barrier, fortress wall, or shielding before it can inflict damage on an enemy.
- Your own skill level as a gamer, and your speed when it comes to selecting, targeting/aiming, and then firing your weapon.

In each weapon category, up to a dozen or more different types of weapons may become accessible to you. Epic Games regularly tweaks the selection of weapons available, as well as the capabilities of each weapon.

© Epic Games, Inc.

A powerful weapon with no ammo is useless. Collect ammo from chests, Supply Drops, Ammo Boxes (shown), that you find lying on the ground, and that you collect from defeated enemies.

Three Tips to Improve Your Shooting Accuracy

© Epic Games, Inc.

Regardless of the weapon you're using, your aim improves when you're crouching down.

© Epic Games, Inc.

While it's often necessary to run or jump while you're firing a weapon, your accuracy improves when you're standing still.

© Epic Games, Inc.

You almost always have an advantage when you're higher up than your opponent and shooting in a downward direction.

Understand How Weapons Are Rated and Categorized

While every weapon has the ability to cause damage and defeat your adversaries, each is rated based on several criteria, including its rarity. Weapons are color-coded with a hue around them to showcase their rarity.

© Epic Games, Inc.

Weapons with a **gray** hue (shown on the previous page) are "Common."

Weapon with a **green** hue are "Uncommon."

Weapons with a **blue** hue are "Rare."

© Epic Games, Inc.

Weapons with a **purple** hue are "Epic."

© Epic Games, Inc.

"Legendary" weapons (with an **orange** hue) are hard to find, extra powerful, and very rare. If you're able to obtain one, grab it!

It is possible to collect several of the same weapon, but each could have a different rarity. So, if you collect two of the same weapon, and one is rare, but the second is legendary, definitely keep the legendary weapon and trade the other for something else when you find a replacement.

The rarity of a weapon contributes heavily to its Damage Per Second (DPS) Rating. Thus, the DPS Rating for a legendary weapon is much higher than the DPS Rating for an identical weapon that has a common rarity, for example.

- **DPS Rating**—This stands for "Damage Per Second." Use this rating to help estimate a weapon's power. It does not take into account things like the accuracy of your aim or the extra damage you can inflict by making a headshot. In general, DPS is calculated by multiplying the damage the weapon can cause by its fire rate.
- **Damage Rating**—A numeric rating based on how much potential damage a weapon can cause per direct hit.
- **Fire Rate**—This refers to the number of bullets fired per second. Some of the most powerful weapons have a slow Fire Rate, so to inflict the most damage, your aim needs to be perfect. Otherwise, during the time between shots, your enemy could move or launch their own counter-attack.
- **MAG (Magazine) Capacity**—This is the total number of ammunition rounds (or bullets) the weapon can hold at once. Reloading a weapon takes valuable time, during which your soldier will be vulnerable to attack. Your enemy could also move, meaning you'll need to re-aim your weapon.
- **Reload Time**—The number of seconds it takes to reload the weapon, assuming you have replacement ammo available. Some of the most powerful weapons have a very slow reload time, so if your shooting accuracy isn't great, you'll be at a disadvantage.

There are plenty of websites, including: IGN.com (www.ign.com/wikis/fortnite/Weapons), Gameskinny.com (www.gameskinny.com/9mt22/complete-fortnite-battle-royale-weapons-stats-list), and RankedBoost.com (https://rankedboost.com/fortnite/best-weapons-tier-list), that provide the current stats for each weapon offered in Fortnite, based on the latest tweaks made to the game. Just make sure, when you look at this information online, that it refers to the most recently released version of Fortnite: Battle Royale.

Choose Your Arsenal Wisely

Based on where you are, what challenges you're currently encountering, and what you anticipate your needs will be, stock your backpack with the weapons and tools you believe you'll need. For example, as you prepare for the final fights at the end of a match, a sniper rifle and grenade/rocket launcher are essential. You'll likely be hiding in your fortress and trying to defeat the final enemies who are hiding in their own fortress. The weapons you use must be able to destroy fortress walls, plus inflict damage on your enemies.

If during those final minutes of a match an enemy rushes you (or uses a Launch Pad to get close quickly), be prepared to engage in close or mid-range combat. Having a Chug Jug (or other HP and shield power-up essentials) on hand could keep you alive if you're harmed in battle.

At any time, your soldier's backpack can hold six items (including the pickaxe). That leaves five slots in which you can carry different types of guns, alternative weapons (such as a Trap, Remote Explosive, or Grenades), and/or loot (such as Med Kits, Chug Jugs, Shield Potions, Bandages, or Slurp Juice). Make smart inventory decisions throughout each match. The Backpack Inventory screen allows you to view what you have, plus organize the backpack's contents.

While your pickaxe is always positioned in the leftmost slot of your backpack, once the other slots are filled, you have the ability to switch around slot positions, making it faster to scroll through and access what you will use most often. This is done from the Backpack Inventory screen, which is accessible during a match.

SECTION 5

DISCOVER TYPES OF LOOT ON THE ISLAND

Just as powerful weapons and ammo can be found throughout the island, a selection of loot is also available. Loot can help boost your HP, increase your shields, or provide additional weapons or tools that will help you stay alive. Epic Games continuously adds new types of loot to the game.

Descriptions of Loot Items

As of May 2018, the following is a list of loot you'll likely encounter on the island. Some items are considered rare, and much harder to find than others.

© Epic Games, Inc.

Apples—You'll discover Apples under trees, scattered randomly around the island. For each Apple that's consumed, a soldier's HP increases by five.

Bandages—Each time a bandage is used, it replenishes 15 HP. A player can carry up to 5 bandages within their backpack in a single slot. It takes several seconds to use bandages, during which time a soldier is vulnerable to attack, so be sure you're well-hidden or protected when using this item.

Boogie Bombs—Toss one of these bombs at an opponent and they'll be forced to dance for 5 seconds while taking damage.

Bush—A bush can be worn by a soldier and used as camouflage. Be sure to crouch down to avoid being seen. If there are other bushes in the area, you'll blend right in. However, a bush offers no protection from attacks. If you start moving while camouflaged by a bush, an adversary will definitely notice and attack. This item is best used outside, when standing still, to avoid being detected by nearby enemies.

© Epic Games, Inc.

Cozy Campfires—Once the Cozy Campfire is activated, any soldiers who stands next to it will gain 2 HP per second for up to 25 seconds (up to 50 HP). The drawback is that a soldier is vulnerable to attack during this time, so activate the campfire after building a protective barrier around yourself and the campfire, or find a secure and secluded place to use it.

If you're playing with teammates, multiple people can take advantage of the campfire's healing powers. When you stand next to the flame, look for the "+" icons that appear so you know it's working.

Chug Jugs—This item takes 15 seconds to drink, during which time a soldier is vulnerable to attack unless he/she's protected. Consuming a Chug Jug restores a soldier's HP *and* shield meter to 100 percent. Drink one of these as you enter into later stages of a match, when survival becomes more difficult.

Clingers—When you throw one of these plunger-shaped grenades at an enemy, it sticks to them and then explodes.

© Epic Games, Inc.

Grenades—Toss a grenade at an enemy, and it'll explode on impact. Direct hits cause the most damage, but even if the grenade lands close to an enemy, damage is still inflicted.

Impulse Grenades—This type of grenade inflicts damage on enemies and throws them into the air, away from the point of impact.

Launch Pads—Activate this item to catapult your solider into the air, and then automatically deploy their glider. You can then guide them around in mid-air for a few seconds. Use this tool, for example, to escape after being engulfed by the storm, or to flee from an attack. It allows you to move great distances quickly. While you're flying, you can still be shot at by enemies.

Small Shield Potions—Consuming this item increases your shield strength by 25, but it takes several seconds to drink, during which time your soldier is vulnerable to attack.

Med Kits—Restore your health to one hundred percent each time a Med Kit (shown on the previous page) is used. It takes ten seconds to use a Med Kit, during which time your solider is vulnerable to attack.

Port-A-Fort—This insta-fort is made of metal, and is instantly built when you activate it. Use it for protection without the need for manual building. It requires no resources.

Included within the Port-A-Fort are tires which allow you to jump to the top of the fort from the inside with ease. In addition to offering protection, the top of a fort provides an ideal vantage point for shooting enemies in any direction.

Don't forget, anytime you find tires on the island, jump onto them and you'll bounce up higher than you can jump yourself.

Remote Explosives—A soldier can carry up to ten of these explosives at once. Activate it one by attaching it to an object, wall, or structure, and then detonate it remotely from any distance away. After setting up a remote explosive, lure your adversary to its location before detonating it. Just make sure you're far enough away to avoid the explosion yourself.

Shield Potions—Each time you drink a Shield Potion, your shield meter increases by fifty (out of one hundred). Drink two in a row to fully activate and replenish your soldier's shields. This item takes several seconds to consume, during which time your soldier is vulnerable to attack.

Slurp Juice—As you drink this item, your HP and shield strength increases by one point every second (for up to 25 seconds). While you're drinking, your soldier must be standing still and is vulnerable to attack.

Traps—Set a Trap on any structure's floor, wall, or ceiling and then leave it. When an opponent accidently activates the hidden Trap, they'll receive mega-damage. Just make sure you don't set off the Trap yourself once you've activated it, or you'll be the one getting hurt! Shown on the left is a Trap waiting to be picked up and placed into the soldier's backpack for later use.

On the right is what a Trap looks like once it's been place on a wall and activated. Typically, you'd place them where an enemy wouldn't see them.

Anytime you explore a crater (at least during Season 4), chances are you'll find **Hop Rocks**. Eat one and for a short time you will be able to jump higher and leap farther. You'll also be protected from harm as a result of a fall.

Clingers look like toilet plungers. Throw them at any object or enemy, and it'll attach. Within a few seconds, BOOM!

Once a Clinger is thrown and attaches to something (in this case a tree), it'll turn blue when activated. It then creates a decent explosion that'll destroy anything in the vicinity and damage (or defeat) enemies.

SECTION 6
WHAT YOU NEED TO KNOW TO BECOME A PRO

Any expert Fortnite player needs to focus on five areas when it comes to fine-tuning their gaming skills. These include:

1. **Exploitation**—Understand the map, where things are, and how to use the different types of terrain to your advantage.

2. **Fighting**—Know how to collect weapons and tools and then choose which one to use based on the enemy soldier(s) you're encountering at any given moment during a match.

3. **Building**—Be able to determine when and where you need to build; what material (wood, stone, or metal) to use; and how to best utilize the structures you build for protection, to increase your visibility, to get yourself higher than your current opponent, or to help you reach an otherwise inaccessible area.

4. **Staying Alive**—Knowing when to fight and when to run or hide, will help keep you alive longer during a match. Based on the tools at your disposal, learn how to hide and then surprise and ambush your enemies, or utilize Traps or Remote Explosives).

5. **Avoiding the Storm**—If you fail to pay attention to the storm, you could easily wind up stuck deep in it, and unable to escape before your HP and shields are depleted. If you must enter into the storm, be sure your HP and Shield Meter are fully charged. Drink a Chug Jug, if possible. This will give you extra time to escape the clutches of the storm.

Know Your Soldier's Capabilities

Knowing how to control your soldier is essential. The more time you in invest playing Fortnite: Battle Royale, the better your muscle memory will become, allowing you to access the appropriate gaming controls quickly and accurately, without having to think too much about it.

The controls used to handle each of a soldier's movements or capabilities vary based on which gaming platform you're using and how you customize the controls.

From the moment your soldier steps foot on the island, he/she has the ability to:

- **Aim and Shoot a Weapon**—A soldier can aim and shoot a weapon while standing still, crouching down, walking, running, or jumping. It's all about timing and aim.
- **Build**—Enter building mode to create or edit walls, stairs/ ramps, or fortresses. Remember, you can't build and use weapons at the same time, so you need to practice quickly switching between combat mode and building mode.
- **Crouch**—Get down on your knees to improve your aim when firing a weapon, to hide behind an object or structure, or to make yourself shorter in order to pass under an object (such as a partially open garage door).
- **Dance**—After a victory, or anytime it's safe, showcase some dance moves. If you see someone dancing during a match, proceed with caution. The enemy could be trying to lure you into a trap or ambush. Access the Emote menu to choose your action, after customizing the options from the Locker Screen before a match.
- **Grab Items**—When you see any item (a weapon, ammo, or loot) on the ground, walk up to it and grab it, assuming you have space in your backpack. If there's no space remaining, you can swap between the item on the ground and the one you're currently holding.

- **Jump**—Leap upwards. Use this to avoid an attack, or to quickly climb onto or over an object.
- **Open Chests or Ammo Boxes**—Walk up to a chest or ammo box and press the appropriate controller/keyboard button to open it. Its contents will spread out on the ground. Pick and choose which items you want to pick up. It may be necessary to swap out items in your backpack to accommodate new or more powerful weapons and loot. In some cases, you'll be required to crouch down in order to open a chest or ammo box, depending on its position.
- **Open/Close Doors**—Instead of smashing through a door, you can open and close it. However, anyone who's around will hear the sound of the door's movement. When you walk up to a door, press the appropriate controller/keyboard button when you see an Open or Close message on the screen.
- **Run**—Travel faster than walking. The noise from your soldier's movement will be louder.

© Epic Games, Inc.

- **Share a Graphic/Emote**—Toss a graphic icon into the air or perform a movement (such as a salute or dance). By completing challenges, you're able to collect and use a wide range of different emotes. Customize what your soldier can do from the Locker screen before a match.

- **Slide Down Hills/Cliffs**—Instead of jumping off a hill (which reduces your HP), you can safely slide down. You can't slide off structures, towers, or buildings. Shields do not protect you against falls.
- **Smashing with the Pickaxe**—Use your pickaxe to smash and collect resources; to break through roofs, walls, floors, or ceilings; or as a close-range weapon. It'll take some time to defeat an enemy, but if you keep moving around and slashing away, you can win a battle.

© Epic Games, Inc.

- **Spray Paint a Tag**—This is yet another way your soldier can express him- or herself during a match. This ability can be unlocked by completing challenges (or purchased from the Item Shop). Leave your painted mark on any surface.

© Epic Games, Inc.

An emote, dance, or spray paint tag is done from this Emote menu screen (shown on the previous page) which is accessible anytime during a match.

The Emotes menu can be customized before any match by accessing the Locker screen and selecting any of the six Emotes slots. Choose what unlocked content you want to include within each slot. This can include a dance move, graphic, or spray paint tag.

- **Tiptoe**—Crouch down to move slowly and much more quietly.
- **Use Loot**—Knowing when and how to use the loot you've collected can keep you alive longer and help you defeat opponents. Be creative when using Traps, Remote Explosives, and Grenades, and don't waste HP or shield power-ups. As soon as you find a power-up that'll activate your shields, use it. Keep your shields as fully charged as possible.
- **Walk**—Move in any direction, at a steady pace. You have full control over the direction your soldier travels. Anytime you move, your soldier's footsteps generate noise.

As for items that will boost your HP, use 'em when you need 'em. Keep in mind that some health and shield power-ups take between five and thirty seconds to consume or utilize, so be sure you're well protected.

Build walls around yourself before drinking a Chug Jug or using a Cozy Campfire, for example, since these take the longest to utilize and leave you exposed. You can't move or do anything else when consuming or using most HP/shield power-ups.

Collect Weapons, Ammo, and Loot from Defeated Soldiers

One of the fastest and easiest ways to build your arsenal and expand your collection of resources during a match is to defeat enemy soldiers and then collect what they leave behind. Just make sure you're well protected when you move in to collect the loot, or another enemy could launch a surprise attack and try to collect what the terminated enemy left behind, as well as what you're carrying if you get defeated as well.

Master the Art of Building

Becoming an expert builder, especially in the heat of battle, requires practice, as well as some creativity when it comes to designing structures. Either by watching livestreams of expert players on YouTube or Twitch.tv, or by staying in Spectator mode after you're eliminated from a match, watch the final stages of matches carefully to learn techniques for building fortresses, and to discover some fort design ideas that work well.

To practice your building technique, travel to an unpopular and unpopulated area of the island, focus on collecting resources, and then fine-tune your building skills. Experiment with different structure designs and develop the skill set needed to be able to build very quickly, without having to think too much about it.

The following are additional strategies to help you become an expert builder:

When building a fortress, cover all sides. Don't forget to build a roof to protect you from assaults from above. Metal is used here, for the first floor of a mini-fortress.

As you're building the foundation of a fort, for example, reinforce the first floor with metal or extra panels. This way, if an enemy manages to sneak up and launch a close-range attack, you'll have extra time to react before your fortress crumbles.

You can use a grenade launcher from a distance to destroy part or all of an enemy fortress, and most types of mid- to long-range shotguns and rifles will also work. However, if you can sneak up on the enemy from the ground, attach a Remote Explosive to the base of their fort, or toss a few grenades. This is typically quicker than continuously shooting at a fortress wall to weaken or destroy it.

© Epic Games, Inc.

In many instances, height is more important than security. Build a quick and tall ramp upwards, and then shoot down at enemies below. Add a vertical wall on both sides of the ramp for added protection. As long as an enemy does not have time to shoot and destroy your ramp while you're at the top of it, you'll be at an advantage. It's safe for your soldier to fall up to three stories when leaping out of a structure you built. If he/she falls from any higher, injury (or worse) will result.

When you need quick protection, build a vertical wall with the strongest material you have available, and then quickly build a ramp (or stairs) directly behind it. You can then crouch down behind this structure for protection. Doing this provides a double layer of shielding that an enemy will have to shoot through or destroy in order to reach you. Plus, by crouching down, you become a smaller target.

Double up on the wall-ramp combo, and then crouch behind it for even greater protection.

© Epic Games, Inc.

In some cases, building two ramps side-by-side gives you an advantage. First, an opponent can't see your exact location when you move back and forth between ramps. Also, if one ramp is about to get destroyed, quickly leap to the other to survive the attack. Yes, this requires more resources, but it's often worth it.

A "ramp rush" is a strategy that involves building a tall ramp quickly, so you're able to move directly toward and over an enemy (or their base) to initiate an attack. Using the double-wide ramp and zigzagging between ramps makes it harder for your enemies to track your exact location.

© Epic Games, Inc.

Smashing wooden pallets (shown on the previous page) often generates more wood than smashing trees. However, trees provide more wood than the walls, floors, and ceilings of houses or buildings. Giant trees, like those found Moisty Mire, tend to generate the most wood. During normal combat, wood is typically the best resource to use. Save your stone and metal for fort building during the final stages of a match.

Harvesting metal from cars and trucks generates the best results, but also creates a ton of noise. Don't forget, when you defeat an enemy, you can collect the weapons and resources (wood, stone, and metal) they leave behind. Defeating two or three enemies during a match will typically allow you to collect more than enough resources without having to harvest too much yourself.

Once you've built one or more walls, instead of wasting time editing the wall to add a window, simply enter Building Mode and face the wall. It will become temporarily transparent. You can see out, but the strength of the wall remains intact for your protection.

© Epic Games, Inc.

Each floor of a basic fort can consist of four walls, with a ramp inside used to reach the next level up. By expanding the width of your fort at various levels, you make it harder for enemies to figure out where you're hiding inside. If opponents have forts taller than yours, or are positioned higher than you, don't forget to add a roof, or keep building onto your fort so it becomes taller.

© Epic Games, Inc.

For enhanced shielding and additional protection against snipers, grenades, and other weapons, place the pyramid-shaped roof structures around the upper perimeter of your fortress.

Consider adding Traps and/or Remote Explosives near the bottom of your fortress, in case an enemy tries to sneak inside to attack you while you're hiding on an upper level of your fort. When you place a Trap, drop some loot below it to lure in enemies.

When your enemy is building a fort close to you, use the same material as them to hide the construction noise, and strive to make your fort taller. Remember, the soldier with the height advantage during a firefight often wins.

If you see a weakness in a tall structure, and you know an enemy is at or near the top of it, shoot at that weak point. Making the structure collapse will cause your enemy to fall. A short fall will have little impact, but a fall from five or more levels up could be devastating.

Learn to Quickly Build "1x1" Fortresses

A 1x1 fortress is simply four walls around you, with a ramp in the center that goes up multiple levels. Using wood allows you to build with the greatest speed, but using metal offers the greatest protection. Keep practicing until you're able to build this type of fortress very quickly, without having to think too much about it.

Here's how to build a 1x1 fortress:

First build four vertical walls so they surround you.

In the center, build a ramp. As the ramp is being constructed (shown on the previous page), jump on it. Keep repeating this process to add levels to your fort.

© Epic Games, Inc.

At the top, consider adding four pyramid-shaped roof pieces around the roof for added protection when you peek out. However, if you need protection from above as well, add a flat roof or a pyramid-shaped roof piece directly over your head.

SECTION 7

PREPARE FOR THE FINAL BATTLES

Those final minutes of a match (known as the "End Game")—when the circle becomes very small and only a few of the most highly skilled enemy soldiers remain alive—are when you'll need to step up and showcase your survival, building, and fightings kills—often at the same time—in order to win the match and become the last person standing.

Step one is to be prepared. Go into the final circle with your HP and Shield Meters fully charged. Plus, have plenty of resources on hand (at least 1,000 to 1,500 wood, stone, and/or metal is ideal). It's also necessary to have the right assortment of weapons in your arsenal. A grenade launcher and/or rocket launcher and a sniper rifle (or rifle with a scope) are definitely must-have weapons.

Never lose sight of your ultimate objective—to be the last person standing at the end of a match.

12 End Game Strategies to Help You Prepare to Win Any Match

Preparation is the key when you enter into the End Game in hopes of winning a match. It's also important to stay calm, watch what your enemies are doing, and stay focused on your objectives.

Here are twelve End Game strategies to help you win:

1. Choose the best location to build your fortress, from which you'll make your final stand in battle. If you're in a good position, you can be more aggressive with your attacks. However, if you're in the dead center of the final circle, you will become the center of attention, which probably isn't good.

2. Make sure your fortress is tall, well-fortified, and that it offers an excellent 360-degree view of the surrounding area from the top level.

3. If your fortress gets destroyed, be prepared to move quickly, and have a backup strategy in place that will help to ensure your survival. Having the element of surprise for your attacks gives you a tactical advantage. Don't become an easy target to hit. Keep moving around your fort, or while you're out in the open!

4. During the End Game, don't engage every remaining player. Allow them to fight among themselves to reduce their numbers, and to reduce or even deplete their ammo and resources.

5. Only rely on a sniper rifle (or scoped rifle) to make long-range shots if you have really good aim. Otherwise use explosive weapons that'll cause damage over a wide area, such as a Grenade Launcher or Rocket Launcher.

6. Always keep tabs on the location of your remaining enemies during the End Game. Don't allow them to sneak up behind you. Even if your back is to the storm, an enemy could enter the storm temporarily, and then emerge behind you to launch a surprise attack if you lose track of

their location. Gamers who use the storm to their tactical advantage are referred to as "storm riders." If you lose track of an enemy whom you know is nearby, listen carefully for their movement.

7. Don't invest a lot of resources in a massive and highly fortified fortress until you know you're in the final circle during a match. Refer to the map and the displayed timer. Otherwise, when the storm expands and moves, you could find it necessary to abandon your fort, and then need to build another one quickly, in a not-so-ideal location. Having to rebuild will use up your resources.

8. Base pushers are enemies who aren't afraid to leave their fortress and attempt to attack yours during the final minutes of a match. Be prepared to deal with their close-range threat.

9. If two or three enemies remain, focus on one at a time. Determine who appears to be the most imminent and greatest threat. Be prepared to change priorities at a moment's notice based on the actions of your enemies.

10. Some final battles take place on ramps, not from within fortresses. In this situation, speed, quick reflexes, getting higher up than your enemy, and good aim with the proper weapon are the keys to winning.

11. Have a Chug Jug on hand to replenish your HP and shields if you're attacked, and incur damage, but are not defeated. Make sure you're well protected when you drink the Chug Jug. Med Kits are also great for maintaining HP during End Games.

12. Study the live streams created by expert Fortnite players (on YouTube and Twitch.tv) to learn their End Game strategies, and see how they react to various challenges.

SECTION 8
FORTNITE RESOURCES

Pro gamers around the world have created YouTube channels, online forums, and blogs focused exclusively on Fortnite: Battle Royale. Plus, you can watch pro players compete online and describe their best strategies or check out the coverage of Fortnite: Battle Royale published by leading gaming websites and magazines.

On YouTube (www.youtube.com) or Twitch.TV (www.twitch.tv/directory /game/Fortnite), in the Search field, enter the search phrase "Fortnite: Battle Royale" to discover many game-related channels, live streams, and pre-recorded videos.

Be sure to check out these awesome online resources that will help you become a better Fortnite: Battle Royale player:

Screenshot from youtube.com. © YouTube. All rights reserved by YouTube

WEBSITE OR YOUTUBE CHANNEL NAME	DESCRIPTION	URL
Epic Games' Fortnite YouTube Channel	The official Fortnite YouTube channel.	www.youtube.com/user/epicfortnite
Epic Games' official Fortnite website	Learn all about Fortnite: Battle Royale, as well as the paid editions of Fortnite.	www.Fortnite.com
Epic Games' official Twitter feed for Fortnite	The official Fortnite Twitter feed.	https://twitter.com/fortnitegame (@fortnitegame)
FantasticalGamer	A popular YouTuber who publishes Fortnite tutorial videos.	www.youtube.com/user/FantasticalGamer
Fandom's Fortnite Wiki	Discover the latest news and strategies related to Fortnite.	http://fortnite.wikia.com/wiki/Fortnite_Wiki
FBR Insider	The Fortnite: Battle Royale Insider website offers game-related news, tips, and strategy videos.	www.fortniteinsider.com
Game Informer Magazine's Fortnite Coverage	Discover articles, reviews, and news about Fortnite published by *Game Informer* magazine.	www.gameinformer.com/search/searchresults.aspx?q=Fortnite
Game Skinny Online Guides	A collection of topic-specific strategy guides related to Fortnite.	www.gameskinny.com/tag/fortnite-guides/
IGN Entertainment's Fortnite Coverage	Check out all IGN's past and current coverage of Fortnite.	www.ign.com/wikis/fortnite
Jason R. Rich's Website and Social Media Feeds	Share your Fortnite gameplay strategies with this book's author and learn about his other books.	www.JasonRich.com Twitter: @JasonRich7 Instagram: @JasonRich7
Microsoft's Xbox One Fortnite Website	Learn about and acquire Fortnite: Battle Royale if you're an Xbox One gamer.	www.microsoft.com/en-US/store/p/Fortnite-Battle-Royale/BT5P2X999VH2

(Continued on next page)

MonsterDface YouTube and Twitch.tv Channels	Watch video tutorials and live game streams from an exert Fortnite player.	www.youtube.com/user/MonsterdfaceLive www.Twitch.tv/MonsterDface
Nomxs	A YouTube and Twitch TV channel hosted by online personality Simon Britton (Nomxs). It features Fortnite game streams.	https://youtu.be/np-8cmsUZmc or www.twitch.tv/videos/259245155
Sony's PS4 Fortnite Website	Learn about and acquire Fortnite if you're a PS4 gamer.	www.playstation.com/en-us/games/fortnite-ps4

Screenshot from Twitch Prime. © Twitch. All rights reserved by Twitch

Point your web browser to Epic Games's Fortnite News page (www.epic-games.com/fortnite/en-US/news) to discover what new features have just been added to Fortnite: Battle Royale, plus get a preview of what's on the way.

Screenshot from IGN.com, © IGN. All rights reserved by IGN

IGN.com offers extensive news and tip-oriented coverage of Fortnite.

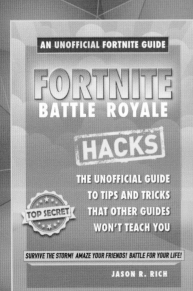

With no two game-play experiences alike, *Fortnite Battle Royale Hacks* will train you to adapt offensive and defensive fighting strategies and boost your chances of survival.

Learn everything you need to know to be the last person standing!

Fortnite Battle Royale Hacks: Secrets of the Island takes a geography-based approach to helping players come out on top, while also providing essential fighting, building, and exploring strategies to make you battle-ready.

Discover everything you need for a *Fortnite* victory!

Your Fortnite Adventure Continues . . .

Epic Games continues to update Fortnite: Battle Royale by making sometimes dramatic alterations to the island map; by introducing challenging new gameplay modes; by revealing exciting new storylines and subplots; by adding powerful new weapons and innovative types of new loot; and by making available eye-catching ways to showcase your soldier's appearance (with outfits, back bling, pickaxes, gliders, emotes, and other customizable elements).

This game continues to evolve, ensuring that it never becomes boring, predictable, or easy to master. Even if you do get really good playing in Solo mode, when you gather one or more friends to compete with you in the Duos or Squads gameplay modes (accessible from the Lobby), the challenges and unpredictability within the game increase dramatically. Teamwork (including constant communication with your allies) becomes important.

Now that you've discovered tons of useful strategies to follow, what will make you a truly awesome gamer is a ton of practice!

Good luck, and more importantly, have fun!

NOTES

HACKS FOR FORTNITE